PRAYERS AT BREAKFAST

Prayers
at Breakfast

by

BERYL BYE

LONDON
LUTTERWORTH PRESS

TO MY FAMILY
whose suggestions and comments
moulded the shape of this book

Printed in Great Britain by
Latimer Trend & Co Ltd, Plymouth

PRAYERS AT BREAKFAST

THE introduction and regular practice of good habits in family life require determination, patience and persistence. Any honest parent is forced to admit this to be true. Even the cleaning of infant teeth and the washing of junior necks becomes a constant battle in which the parent is sometimes tempted to lay down arms and say "Does it matter?"

Why, therefore, should we expect to find the introduction of family prayers into our daily life any less difficult? While one presumes the Devil is not greatly concerned with healthy teeth and clean necks, he is vastly concerned with healthy Christians and clean lives and we must therefore be prepared for opposition.

Once the habit of praying together at the breakfast table for a few minutes every day has been introduced, the first hurdle has been cleared and we only need to develop our staying power.

We find that prayers before breakfast is the best arrangement for only then is the family unit likely to remain intact. Sudden evacuations to catch buses or trains, collect games kit, clean shoes, and other emergencies tend to interrupt after-breakfast prayers.

With children under three it is a good idea to present them with a rusk or bowl of cereal just as you are due to commence prayers. After all, there is no point in trying to compete vocally with an outraged toddler demanding sustenance.

In time (children being born mimics) they will put down their spoon at the appropriate point, angelically fold their hands and repeat a loud *amen*! This is our experience with our three-year-old.

From four upwards children will enjoy family prayers much more if we let them take an active part. One can read the verses, another say the prayers and yet another contribute to the grace, while the whole family try to decide upon "the thought" without looking!

"Prayers at Breakfast" are specially designed for the modern, lively and talkative family, and only take a very few minutes, but they do ensure that meeting with God becomes a regular good habit.

Can you and your family afford to neglect it?

Note: The eleventh—fourteenth weeks in this book are suitable for reading during the last four weeks of Lent, and readers may like to reserve them for this time; they will, of course, only occasionally coincide of their own accord. It is suggested that in many instances the readings should be taken from one of the modern Bible translations such as the Revised Standard Version, the New English Bible or Phillips.

B.B.

ACKNOWLEDGEMENTS

THE author is indebted to the Religious Education Press Ltd, Wallington, Surrey, for permission to reproduce graces from their publication, *Prayers and Graces*, collected by Mary Sharp. These include verses and a translation by Jane M. Campbell, J. M. Macdougall Ferguson, E. Rutter Leatham and R. J. Weston. She is also grateful to the editor of *The Church of England Newspaper* for permission to use prayers and graces which appeared originally in his columns.

Grace for the Week:

Give us grateful and thankful hearts for this food that is set before us now, O Lord. Amen.

Monday:

Reading: St. Matthew 2: 12–15.

Thought: God's warnings should be heeded.

Prayer: Dear God, give us listening ears that hear Your warnings against wrong thoughts and actions, and teach us always to heed Your Voice. Amen.

Tuesday:

Reading: St. Matthew 2: 19–21.

Thought: God can remove obstacles.

Prayer: Heavenly Father, make our paths straight and plain and remove anything that may hinder Your will. Amen.

Wednesday:

Reading: St. John 13: 34–35.

Thought: A new commandment for a New Year.

Prayer: We think today, Lord Jesus, of the new commandment You gave to us—help us to live it out in our lives in the New Year that lies ahead. Amen.

Thursday:

Reading: St. Matthew 2: 22–23.

Thought: God directs our movements.

Prayer: Dear God, You have shown us from Your Book how Joseph was directed about his journeys and the place where he should make his home. Direct our journeyings and dwell in our homes, we pray You. Amen.

Friday:

Reading: St. Luke 2: 41–45.

Thought: Do we ever fail to find the Lord Jesus?

Prayer: Lord Jesus, when it seems as if we have lost You, reassure us of Your presence with us always, we pray You. Amen.

Saturday:

Reading: St. Luke 2: 46–49.

Thought: Is it natural for our children to be found in God's House?

Prayer: Dear Lord Jesus, as our children grow older may we always find them in God's House on His Day. Amen.

Sunday:

Reading: St. Luke 2: 50–52.

Thought: Are we growing in the love of God?

Prayer: Dear Father God, help us day by day to grow in the love of the Lord, so that others may love us because of Your likeness. Amen.

Grace for the Week:

Let us pause a moment
To thank our God above,
Who gives to us His children
These countless gifts of love.

Monday:

Reading: St. Matthew 5: 1–4.

Thought: Earth's poverty is heaven's riches.

Prayer: O Lord, help us to work for the riches of the kingdom of heaven which will never pass away. Amen.

Tuesday:

Reading: St. Matthew 5: 5–8.

Thought: Do we really "hunger" after goodness?

Prayer: O Lord Jesus, give us a real hunger for goodness and fill us with Your Holy Spirit, we pray You. Amen.

Wednesday:

Reading: St. Matthew 5: 9–12.

Thought: Can we "rejoice" when we are unjustly accused?

Prayer: O Lord God, sometimes You know we are unjustly judged for something that is not our fault. Help us to take it patiently for Your sake. Amen.

Thursday:

Reading: St. Matthew 5: 13.

Thought: Are we fresh or stale "salt"?

Prayer: O God, we know how useful salt is in our daily lives. Make us just as useful to those with whom we live and work and play. Amen.

Friday:

Reading: St. Matthew 5: 14–16.

Thought: Is our light shining for God?

Prayer: Let our light so shine before men, that they may see our good works and glorify our Father which is in heaven. Amen.

Saturday:

Reading: St. Matthew 5: 34–37.

Thought: Is our language pleasing to God?

Prayer: O God, teach us to think before we speak so that all our words may be pleasing to You. Amen.

Sunday:

Reading: Matthew 5: 38–42.

Thought: Do we go the extra "mile"?

Prayer: Loving Lord Jesus, give us the love and grace to forgive those who would quarrel with us, and to serve those who we feel least deserve our help. Amen.

Grace for the Week:

We thank you, Lord, for this good food. Be with us as we eat it, and stay with each one of us throughout the coming day. In Your name we ask it. Amen.

Monday:

Reading: Matthew 5: 43–45.

Thought: Do we follow this rule for living?

Prayer: Dear Father God, help us to love and not to hate. Help us to bless and not to curse. Help us to pray for, and do good to those who give us cause to dislike them. Amen.

Tuesday:

Reading: Matthew 5: 46–48.

Thought: Holy "huddles" are useless!

Prayer: Gracious Lord, we thank you for our special friends within our church, but teach us to love and exchange greetings with those outside our own circle, so that we may bring them in. Amen.

Wednesday:

Reading: Matthew 6: 1–4.

Thought: Is our giving secret?

Prayer: O God, show us this day a good deed or a generous gift that we can do or give for You, and help us to keep it secret from everyone else. Amen.

Thursday:

Reading: Matthew 6: 5–6.

Thought: Are our prayer private?

Prayer: O Lord Jesus, we confess how scanty and hasty are our private prayers. Give us a fresh longing to speak to You every day. Amen.

Friday:

Reading: Matthew 6: 7–13.

Thought: Do we sometimes use the Lord's prayer thoughtlessly?

Prayer: Our Father, Which art in heaven, hallowed be Thy Name. Thy kingdom come. Thy will be done in earth as it is in heaven. Give us this day our daily bread and forgive us our trespasses, as we forgive those that trespass against us. Lead us not into temptation but deliver us from evil, for Thine is the Kingdom, the Power and the Glory, for ever and ever. Amen.

Saturday:

Reading: Matthew 6: 14–15.

Thought: Dare we claim God's forgiveness?

Prayer: O Lord Jesus, Who took our punishment so that we might be forgiven, help us to forgive as You do. Amen.

Sunday:

Reading: Matthew 6: 19–21.

Thought: Does our bank balance need mothballs?

Prayer: O God, Who has given to us more than we would have dared to ask, make us generous with everything that we have, for we know that we have it only in trust for You. Amen.

Grace for the Week:

All good gifts around us,
Are sent from heaven above;
Then thank the Lord, O thank the
  Lord,
For all His Love.   Amen.

Monday:

Reading: Matthew 6: 24–26.

Thought: Who is our Master?

Prayer: Our Lord and Master, give us a simple trust in You and help us not to worry about our daily needs, for if we are faithful servants we know that You will provide for us.   Amen.

Tuesday:

Reading: Matthew 6: 27–34.

Thought: God knows that clothes are a necessity.

Prayer: O God our Father, when we put on our warm clothes each morning, make us thankful for them, and give us a concern to help those of our brothers who are not so warmly clad.   Amen.

Wednesday:

Reading: Matthew 6: 31–34.

Thought: Do we live one day at a time?

Prayer: O Lord, we know we so often worry about things that may never happen. Help us to live one day at a time, and to live it unto You.   Amen.

Thursday:

Reading: Matthew 7: 1–5.

Thought: Are we more concerned with other people's faults than our own?

Prayer: O Lord Jesus, we confess how quickly we see other people's faults, and how slow we are to recognize our own. Forgive us, and make us more forgiving. Amen.

Friday:

Reading: Matthew 7: 7–11.

Thought: When we ask, do we expect to receive?

Prayer: O God our Father, give us the faith to expect an answer to our prayers.   Amen.

Saturday:

Reading: Matthew 7: 12–14.

Thought: Which "gate" have we chosen?

Prayer: Loving Saviour, lead us through the narrow gate and along the hard way, because we know it is the only way to heaven.   Amen.

Sunday:

Reading: Matthew 7: 15–18.

Thought: Is our fruit good or bad?

Prayer: We know, O Lord, that we are judged by the way we behave. Help us to bring forth good fruit and bring glory to Your Name.   Amen.

Grace for the Week:

God who is kind and good,
Gives us our daily food.
Let us not fail to say
"Thank You" to Him each day.
                    Amen.

Monday:

Reading: Exodus 20: 1–3.
  Thought: Put God first.
  Prayer: Dear Father God, help us always to put You first in all we do. Amen.

Tuesday:

Reading: Exodus 20: 4–6.
  Thought: God alone deserves worship.
  Prayer: Dear God, accept our worship as we bow before You now, and direct it into the right channels. Amen.

Wednesday:

Reading: Exodus 20: 7.
  Thought: Are we guiltless?
  Prayer: Cleanse our lips, dear Lord, and use them to speak good things. Amen.

Thursday:

Reading: Exodus 20: 8–11.
  Thought: How do we use the Sabbath day?
  Prayer: Help us to use aright, dear God, the day You have given to us for rest and worship. Amen.

Friday:

Reading: Exodus 20: 12.
  Thought: Do we honour our parents?
  Prayer: Our heavenly Father, help us to give our earthly parents our respect and love, and to be observant of their needs. Amen.

Saturday:

Reading: Exodus 20: 13–16.
  Thought: God's laws are never out of date.
  Prayer: Dear God, may we keep Your laws ever before us, so that we do not fall into grievous sin. Amen.

Sunday:

Reading: Exodus 20: 17.
  Thought: Do we recognize covetousness as sin?
  Prayer: Dear Father in heaven, make us content with what we have, for if we have the Lord Jesus for our Saviour, we have earth's greatest treasure. Amen.

Grace for the Week:

For healthy appetites, and the means to satisfy them, we thank You, Lord. Amen.

Monday:

Reading: Genesis 37: 1–2.

Thought: Do we tell tales?

Prayer: Lord Jesus, we confess how easily we complain of other people's wrongdoing. Forgive us and help us to keep silent when it is wise to do so. Amen.

Tuesday:

Reading: Genesis 37: 3–4.

Thought: Jealousy and hatred go hand in hand.

Prayer: O God, we ask you to free us from the sin of jealousy which so often leads to hate and disunity. For the sake of the Lord Jesus, our King of Love, we ask it. Amen.

Wednesday:

Reading: Genesis 37: 5–7.

Thought: A still tongue makes a wise head!

Prayer: Heavenly Father, we realize how much of our conversation is unprofitable and useless. Help us to choose our words with tact and love. Amen.

Thursday:

Reading: Genesis 37: 8–10.

Thought: We don't always learn by our mistakes.

Prayer: O God, so often we fail to learn from our mistakes and continue to repeat them. Give us Your grace to conquer our besetting sins. Amen.

Friday:

Reading: Genesis 37: 11–14.

Thought: Are we willing messengers?

Prayer: O Lord, make us willing to bear Your message to those of our own family to whom it may be Your will to send us. Amen.

Saturday:

Reading: Genesis 37: 18–20.

Thought: Are we ever deliberately unkind?

Prayer: O Lord Jesus, we confess that we are sometimes deliberately unkind to other people. Forgive us and help us to show them Your love. Amen.

Sunday:

Reading: Genesis 37: 21–22.

Thought: Are we content with half-measures?

Prayer: O Father God, give us the courage to refuse to have anything to do with plans that may hurt someone else, so that we may be worthy to be called Your disciples. Amen.

Grace for the Week:

We thank Thee, loving Father,
For all Thy tender care;
For food and clothes and shelter,
And all Thy world so fair.
                    Amen.

Monday:

Reading: Genesis 37: 23–25.

Thought: No situation is hopeless.

Prayer: O God our Father, when things seem at their worst, and there appears to be no way out of a difficulty—teach us even then to trust in You. Amen.

Tuesday:

Reading: Genesis 37: 26–28.

Thought: There is no profit in evil.

Prayer: O Lord, show us that we never gain any true profit from evil, and contentment only comes from doing Your will. Amen.

Wednesday:

Reading: Genesis 37: 29–31.

Thought: We should be careful to whom we go for advice.

Prayer: O God, when we ask for advice on important problems, remind us to seek it from those who know You. Amen.

Thursday:

Reading: Genesis 37: 32–34.

Thought: Don't jump to conclusions!

Prayer: O Lord, so often we are ready to believe the worst. Make us wary of over-quick decisions. Amen.

Friday:

Reading: Genesis 37: 35–36.

Thought: Some people are happy in their misery!

Prayer: O God, we know there is a time to weep, and a time to cease from weeping. Save us from the sin of self-pity. Amen.

Saturday:

Reading: Genesis 39: 1–3.

Thought: The most humble task can be done for Jesus.

Prayer: In all we do
    At home, at school, at play,
In all we are
    And all we think and say,
May others see
Just Jesus all the way. Amen.

Sunday:

Reading: Genesis 39: 4–5.

Thought: Good work never goes unnoticed.

Prayer: O Lord, may our work always be done well, so that others may be able to trust us because we are known as Your servants. Amen.

Grace for the Week:

For sleep to refresh us,
For a family to love us,
And for food to satisfy our hunger,
We thank You, Lord.   Amen.

Monday:

Reading: Job 1: 1–3.
   Thought: Are we perfect and upright?
   Prayer: Help us to respect You and turn away from evil so that we may live clean and straight lives, O God.   Amen.

Tuesday:

Reading: Job 1: 4–5.
   Thought: Do we rise early to worship God?
   Prayer: O God, help us to rise early in the morning so that we have time to worship You before the day begins.   Amen.

Wednesday:

Reading: Job 1: 6–8.
   Thought: God delights to see our good actions.
   Prayer: O God our Father, remind us that You see all that we do and hear all that we say, and that You delight to see us living uprightly.   Amen.

Thursday:

Reading: Job 1: 9–12.
   Thought: It's easy to be a Christian when things go well.
   Prayer: Dear Lord, we thank you for the way You have blessed and protected us.   If troubles and difficulties come into our lives, help us to continue to trust in You.   Amen.

Friday:

Reading: Job 1: 13–16.
   Thought: Could we face loss of possessions?
   Prayer: O God, help us to hold the things of this world lightly, so that their loss may not affect our faith in You.   Amen.

Saturday:

Reading: Job 1: 17–19.
   Thought: Could we face bereavement?
   Prayer: O God, please be very close to all those who are mourning the loss of a loved one today. Be Thou their comfort and their strength.   Amen.

Sunday:

Reading: Job 1: 20–22.
   Thought: Are we as faithful as Job?
   Prayer: We thank you, Lord, for all Your servants who stand firm under trials and sorrows and difficulties. Help us to be like them, we pray You.   Amen.

Grace for the Week:

Gratefully we bow our heads
And pause again to say
Thank You for the wholesome food
Which You supply each day.
                    Amen.

Monday:

Reading: Galatians 6: 1–2.

Thought: Do we criticize or help?

Prayer: O Lord, help us to bear one another's burdens and so fulfil the law of Christ. Amen.

Tuesday:

Reading: Galatians 6: 7–8.

Thought: We can only reap what we have sown.

Prayer: God our Father, help us to sow in this life the seeds of good works so that our harvest may be a plentiful one. Amen.

Wednesday:

Reading: Galatians 6: 9–10.

Thought: Do we look for opportunities, or expect them to find us?

Prayer: Lord Jesus, show us those of Your family who need our help so that we may have the opportunity of giving it. Amen.

Thursday:

Reading: 1 John 2: 3–5.

Thought: Do we show our love by our obedience?

Prayer: Our Father, help us to show our love for You by our constant obedience to Your laws. Amen.

Friday:

Reading: 1 John 2: 15–17.

Thought: Have we made our choice?

Prayer: O Lord Jesus, we know we have to choose between the fleeting pleasures of this world and the lasting joys of the next. Help us to make our choice with wisdom. Amen.

Saturday:

Reading: 1 John 3: 16–18.

Thought: Do we shut our eyes to our "brother's" want?

Prayer: O God, open our eyes to the wants of our fellow men, and open our hearts and purses to meet those needs. Amen.

Sunday:

Reading: 1 John 4: 7–11.

Thought: Love should express itself in deeds.

Prayer: Heavenly Father, You showed Your love to us by giving the Lord Jesus to die for our sins. May we express our love by sacrificing ourselves for others. Amen.

Grace for the Week:

Thank You for the world so sweet,
Thank You for the food we eat,
Thank You for the birds that sing,
Thank You, God, for everything.
                              Amen.

Monday:

Reading: Proverbs 3: 1–6.

Thought: God is the only reliable Guide.

Prayer: O Lord, may others see that we love You, by the way we live every day.   Amen.

Tuesday:

Reading: Proverbs 3: 7–10.

Thought: God deserves the first share of all that we have.

Prayer: Give us generous hearts, O God, to give back to You something of what You have given to us.   Amen.

Wednesday:

Reading: Proverbs 3: 11–12.

Thought: Difficulties are sometimes good for us.

Prayer: When we feel that everything is against us, help us to remember that You are for us. Amen.

Thursday:

Reading: Proverbs 3: 27–31.

Thought: Be quick to help, and slow to anger.

Prayer: Make us helpful and free in giving to all those with whom we come in contact at home, at work or at school. Amen.

Friday:

Reading: Proverbs 4: 23–27.

Thought: Our bodies should be God's temple.

Prayer: Take our lips and speak through them, take our minds and think through them, take our hearts and set them on fire with love for Thee. In Thy Name, we ask it.   Amen.

Saturday:

Reading: Proverbs 20: 11–13.

Thought: Does OUR work recommend us?

Prayer: Lord Jesus, may all our works be pure and may our ears be quick to hear Your voice. Amen.

Sunday:

Reading: Proverbs 22: 1–6.

Thought: What kind of riches do WE seek?

Prayer: Dear Lord, help us to choose honesty and uprightness, rather than worldly wealth or gain.   Amen.

Grace for the Week:

Be present at our table, Lord,
Be here and everywhere adored,
Please bless our food, and grant that
*   we*
May feast in Paradise with Thee.
                              Amen.

Monday:

Reading: Luke 21: 1-4.

Thought: Does our Christian giving "hurt" us?

Prayer: Lord, teach us to give generously of our time, our money, and our love, and help us to remember that You gave Your life for us. Amen.

Tuesday:

Reading: Luke 22: 1-5.

Thought: Evil has to be worked through human people.

Prayer: O God, keep us pure in thought and deed so that we may never lend ourselves to the cause of evil. Amen.

Wednesday:

Reading: Luke 22: 24-26.

Thought: Are we always contented to serve?

Prayer: Lord Jesus, help us to find true joy in serving our families and our friends, because we know that in serving them we are serving Thee. Amen.

Thursday:

Reading: Luke 22: 31-34.

Thought: Actions speak louder than words.

Prayer: Heavenly Father, give us Your strength to carry out those things that we know to be right, because we know that without You we can do nothing. Amen.

Friday:

Reading: Luke 22: 39-42.

Thought: Have we learned to pray the prayer of Jesus?

Prayer: Lord Jesus, we would pray Your prayer—"Not our will but Your will"—help us to remember this today, whenever we want our own way. Amen.

Saturday:

Reading: Luke 22: 45-46.

Thought: How often do we "sleep" when we should be praying?

Prayer: Our Father God, forgive us our lack of prayer and teach us how to pray and what to ask for. Amen.

Sunday:

Reading: Luke 22: 47-48.

Thought: Are we sometimes disloyal to our friends?

Prayer: Father in heaven, Who has given us friends to share our joys and our sorrows, help us to be loyal to them at all times. Amen.

17

Grace for the Week:

Lord, we ask that You will bless this food, and supply the needs of those in want. For Jesus' sake.
Amen

Monday:

Reading: Luke 22: 49–51.

Thought: Wrongs can never be righted by violence.

Prayer: Lord Jesus, help us to check the harsh word and the angry blow and to obey Your commands to return good for evil. Amen.

Tuesday:

Reading: Luke 22: 54–58.

Thought: How often do we deny Jesus?

Prayer: O Lord, if today we have a chance to own You as our Lord, give us the courage to do so. Amen.

Wednesday:

Reading: Luke 22: 61–62.

Thought: Tears often come too late.

Prayer: O God, save us from tears that come too late to wash away the consequences of our lack of faith or love or loyalty. Amen.

Thursday:

Reading: Luke 22: 66–71.

Thought: Are we guilty of unbelief?

Prayer: O Lord Jesus, Who came to live as a man in an earthly home so that we might believe and understand Your words; increase our faith and forgive us our unbelief, we pray You. Amen.

Friday:

Reading: Luke 23: 4–7.

Thought: Do we sometimes try to avoid making decisions?

Prayer: O God, give us a clear mind to see the right way, and grant us the strength to follow it. Amen.

Saturday:

Reading: Luke 23: 8–9.

Thought: Jesus wants us to love Him for what He is, not for what He can do.

Prayer: Lord Jesus, may we love You more every day because we know that whatever happens You will always love us. Amen.

Sunday:

Reading: Luke 23: 20–24.

Thought: Can we be persuaded to do what we know to be wrong?

Prayer: Father in heaven, be very near us when we are tempted to take the easy way out, and keep our feet firmly upon Your path. We ask it in Jesus' Name. Amen.

Grace for the Week:

For health, and food, and all Thy gifts,
Lord, we thank Thee. Amen.

Monday:

Reading: Luke 23: 32–34.

Thought: Are we always quick to forgive?

Prayer: Our Father, Which art in heaven, forgive us our trespasses as we forgive them that trespass against us. Amen.

Tuesday:

Reading: Luke 23: 35–37.

Thought: Jesus couldn't save Himself, and us.

Prayer: O dear Lord Jesus, Who gave Yourself for us, take our lives and use them in Your service. Amen.

Wednesday:

Reading: Luke 23: 38–43.

Thought: Do not blame the Lord Jesus—claim His forgiveness.

Prayer: Lord Jesus Christ, forgive us when we blame You for troubles and difficulties that we have so often brought upon ourselves; and use our troubles to bring us nearer to You. Amen.

Thursday:

Reading: Luke 23: 44–47.

Thought: The death of Jesus glorified God—do our lives do the same?

Prayer: O Lord, Who by Your death opened for us the way to heaven: help us by our lives to show others the way to You. Amen.

Friday:

Reading: Luke 23: 49–53.

Thought: While many wondered what to do—Joseph of Arimathea DID something!

Prayer: Lord, please show us some practical way in which we can serve You today. Amen.

Saturday:

Reading: Luke 24: 1–8.

Thought: How many of Jesus' words do WE remember?

Prayer: O God, help us to love Your Book and to read it with understanding, so that we may remember Your words in times of trouble. Amen.

Sunday:

Reading: Luke 24: 8–11.

Thought: We shouldn't doubt miracles just because they've never happened to us!

Prayer: Dear Lord Jesus, may we learn the joy of sharing our experiences of You, so that our own faith may be made stronger. Amen.

Grace for the Week:

Heavenly Father kind and good,
Who dost give Thy children food:
Accept the thanks we gladly bring,
Thanks to God for everything.
                                    Amen.

Monday:

Reading: Luke 24: 13–16.

Thought: Do we always recognize the voice of our Lord?

Prayer: Blessed Lord, You speak to us in so many different ways: teach us to recognize Your voice at all times. Amen.

Tuesday:

Reading: Luke 24: 17–20.

Thought: Sometimes it is wiser to listen to Jesus than to talk to Him!

Prayer: O Lord, we confess today how often we speak to You and do not pause to listen for Your answer. Speak to us now, as we are quiet before You. Amen.

Wednesday:

Reading: Luke 24: 25–27.

Thought: Jesus can help us to understand the hardest passages in the Bible.

Prayer: O God, we thank you for the Bible, and all it means to us. Open our eyes so that we may see the wonderful things in Thy Word. Amen.

Thursday:

Reading: Luke 24: 28–31.

Thought: Blessed is the table when Jesus is the guest.

Prayer: O Lord, help us to remember that: "Christ is the Head of this house, the Unseen Guest at every meal, the Silent Listener to every conversation." Amen.

Friday:

Reading: Luke 24: 36–40.

Thought: Jesus always brings peace and comfort.

Prayer: Dear Lord, in all the rush and bustle of our lives today, in all our goings out and comings in, we pray: give us that inward peace that nothing takes away. Amen.

Saturday:

Reading: Luke 24: 41–45.

Thought: How much proof do we need of the resurrection of Jesus?

Prayer: O Lord Jesus, we thank You for the glory of Your rising from the dead, and Your promise that we may share in Your eternal life. Amen.

Sunday:

Reading: Luke 24: 46–48.

Thought: Christians are still Christ's only witnesses.

Prayer: Lord Jesus: "Let our light so shine before men that they may see our good works, and glorify our Father which is in heaven." Amen.

Grace for the Week:

For all Thy many gifts of food and
drink,
    And special joy of loving com-
    pany,
We bow our heads, and of Thy
    goodness think
    And say a grateful "Thank You"
    unto Thee.

Monday:

Reading: Acts 2: 1–4.

Thought: With God's Spirit we can do the impossible.

Prayer: O Father God, give us Your Holy Spirit within us so that we can do great works for You. Amen.

Tuesday:

Reading: Acts 2: 12–13.

Thought: It is silly to laugh just because we don't understand.

Prayer: O Lord Jesus, there are so many things in the Bible that we don't fully understand. May we never be guilty of mocking at them. Amen.

Wednesday:

Reading: Acts 2: 37–39.

Thought: Peter's words are true for us.

Prayer: Father in heaven, we are sorry for our wrongdoing, please forgive us and give us Your Holy Spirit to help us every day. Amen.

Thursday:

Reading: Acts 2: 41–42.

Thought: There is always something new we can learn.

Prayer: Lord Jesus, may we always find something new to learn about You. Help us to continue Your faithful soldiers and servants unto our lives' end. Amen.

Friday:

Reading: Acts 2: 43–47.

Thought: How do we show the world that we are Christians?

Prayer: O Lord, help us to share what we have with others, whether it be our meals, our money, or our possessions. Amen.

Saturday:

Reading: Acts 3: 1–6.

Thought: Do others look to us for help?

Prayer: Our Father, show us how we can serve other people so that they never look to us for help in vain. Amen.

Sunday:

Reading: Acts 3: 7–10.

Thought: Do people notice a change for the better in us?

Prayer: O Lord Jesus, Who wonderfully changed the life of a lame beggar, change our lives so that others may wonder, and want to seek You for themselves. Amen.

Grace for the Week:

Bless, O Lord, this food to our use,
And ourselves in Thy Service.
For Jesus' sake. Amen.

Monday:

Reading: Acts 4: 5–10.
Thought: Who gets the praise for *our* good deeds?
Prayer: Father, make us bold to witness to the works that You have done, giving all the praise and credit to our Lord, Your own dear Son. Amen.

Tuesday:

Reading: Acts 4: 18–20.
Thought: Do we care what people think more than what God thinks?
Prayer: O Lord, help us to care less what other people think about our words and actions, and more about what *You* think. Amen.

Wednesday:

Reading: Acts 4: 32–35.
Thought: There is no need for anyone to be in need.
Prayer: Our Father, Who has given to us more than we need, give us the spirit of generosity so that we may see and meet the needs of others. Amen.

Thursday:

Reading: Acts 7: 59–60.
Thought: How readily do we forgive?
Prayer: O Lord, we thank You for those of Your servants who can follow Your example of forgiveness in such great ways. Give us more forgiving natures in the little things of life. Amen.

Friday:

Reading: Acts 8: 1–4.
Thought: Sometimes God allows evil so that good may come out of it.
Prayer: O God, Who has set us in a country where we may speak freely of You and Your works—make us ready to pass on the Good News of Your message, whenever we have the chance. Amen.

Saturday:

Reading: Acts 8: 25–27a.
Thought: Do we obey God's voice without question?
Prayer: O Lord, give us quick ears and ready hearts to obey You when You speak to us. Amen.

Sunday:

Reading: Acts 8: 27–31.
Thought: Are we as willing to learn as to teach?
Prayer: O God our Father, make us willing to learn from those who know You best, so that our knowledge of You may grow more every day. Amen.

Grace for the Week:

Father, we thank Thee for the night,
And for the pleasant morning light;
For rest and food and loving care,
And all that makes the day so fair.
                              Amen.

Monday:

Reading: Acts 8: 32–35.

Thought: The Bible is the best starting point in the Christian life.

Prayer: O God, we thank You for Your Wonderful Book from which we learn all we need to know about You. Help us to read it more and understand it better. Amen.

Tuesday:

Reading: Acts 8: 36–39.

Thought: All Christians should have joyful hearts.

Prayer: O Lord, give us a heart so full of joy, that wherever we go, whatever we do and whoever we meet, our happiness may show Your presence within us. Amen.

Wednesday:

Reading: Acts 9: 1–6.

Thought: When we are unkind to others we are unkind to Jesus.

Prayer: Lord Jesus, forgive us for hard words and unkind actions, for we know that whatever we do unto others, we do unto You. Amen.

Thursday:

Reading: Acts 9: 10–12.

Thought: We too can be the answer to someone's prayer.

Prayer: O Father God, perhaps today someone will pray a prayer for help to which *we* can be the answer. We are here Lord if You need us. Amen.

Friday:

Reading: Acts 9: 13–16.

Thought: God can change sinners into saints.

Prayer: O God, Who can change the hearts of all men, change our hearts and fill them with love to all men. Amen.

Saturday:

Reading: Acts 9: 17–19.

Thought: Could we call our greatest enemy "brother"?

Prayer: O Lord, we think now of the person we love the least. Give us Your grace to think of him as our brother. Amen.

Sunday:

Reading: Acts 9: 20–22.

Thought: Forget evil and remember good.

Prayer: Lord Jesus, help us to forgive and forget the wrongs that others have done and to remember only their kindnesses. Amen.

Grace for the Week:

You have sent this food, Dear God, to make our bodies healthy and strong. We bow our heads now and say "We thank You, God".

Amen.

Monday:

Reading: Acts 9: 23–27.

Thought: God can protect us from danger.

Prayer: O God, we give into Your safe keeping today all those we love. Guard and protect them and us, we pray You. Amen.

Tuesday:

Reading: Acts 9: 36–39.

Thought: Will people remember us for our kindly actions?

Prayer: O Lord, help us to serve You by serving other people in whatever way we can. Amen.

Wednesday:

Reading: Acts 9: 40–42.

Thought: Do we remember to pray before we act?

Prayer: Remind us, Lord, that we need Your strength before we can do any great work for You. Amen.

Thursday:

Reading: Acts 12: 1–5.

Thought: Some people are still imprisoned for their faith.

Prayer: O God, we pray today for all those people who at this time are imprisoned for their faith. May Your angels be very near them, we pray You. Amen.

Friday:

Reading: Acts 12: 6–10.

Thought: God can make our heart's dreams come true.

Prayer: O God, You know the secret longings of our hearts, make them come true if they will bring glory to Your name. Amen.

Saturday:

Reading: Acts 12: 11–16.

Thought: Do we expect prayers to be answered?

Prayer: O God, when we pray in Your Name, give us faith to believe that our prayers will be answered. Amen.

Sunday:

Reading: Acts 14: 8–10.

Thought: Are we grateful for our good health?

Prayer: O God, Who has given to us the precious gift of good health, make us specially thoughtful to all those who are crippled or ill in any way. Amen.

Grace for the Week:

For what we are about to receive, may the Lord make us truly thankful. Amen.

Monday:

Reading: Ruth 1: 1–5.

Thought: In times of sorrow, Jesus can be *our* comfort.

Prayer: O God, we ask You to be today with all who mourn the loss of a loved one. Give them Your courage, and Your strength. Amen.

Tuesday:

Reading: Ruth 1: 6–9.

Thought: Even in her own sorrow, Naomi was able to comfort.

Prayer: O Lord, help us to put aside our own trials and difficulties, so that we may be a help to others. Amen.

Wednesday:

Reading: Ruth 1: 10–14.

Thought: Unselfish love wants the best for others, not for ourselves.

Prayer: O God, give us the kind of love that cares more about others than ourselves. Amen.

Thursday:

Reading: Ruth 1: 15–18.

Thought: When we are sure of the right path to take, let us keep to it.

Prayer:
Show us the path to take,
Be Thou alone our Guide,
And give us strength, steep hills to climb.
If Thou be at our side.
Amen.

Friday:

Reading: Ruth 1: 19–22.

Thought: Our words are our witness.

Prayer: O God, when things go wrong and we blame You, forgive us, we pray You, and strengthen our faith so that we can say "Thy will be done". Amen.

Saturday:

Reading: Ruth 2: 1–3.

Thought: Ruth was a worker, not a drone!

Prayer: O Lord, help each one of us to work willingly at school, at home, or at work. Amen.

Sunday:

Reading: Ruth 2: 3–9.

Thought: The more we have ourselves, the more we should give away.

Prayer: O Lord Jesus, Who had no earthly possessions to give away, and so gave Yourself for us, make us mindful of the needs of others and quick to help them. Amen.

Grace for the Week:

Lord bless this food which now we take,
And make us strong, for Jesus' sake.
                                    Amen.

Monday:

Reading: Ruth 2: 10–13.

Thought: A friendly word is worth a lot.

Prayer: O God, show us a newcomer to our schools, our work, or our district, to whom we can give a friendly word.
                                    Amen.

Tuesday:

Reading: Ruth 2: 14–17.

Thought: We need to be tactful in the way we give.

Prayer: Heavenly Father, let us take pleasure in giving secretly, so that those that receive may give You all the praise, and all the glory. Amen.

Wednesday:

Reading: Ruth 2: 18–23.

Thought: God's goodness overcame Naomi's bitterness.

Prayer: O God, may the knowledge of Your care fill us with praise and thankfulness. Amen.

Thursday:

Reading: Ruth 3: 1–6.

Thought: Sometimes it is right to obey, even if we don't fully understand why we should!

Prayer: O God, You know what is best for us much better than we know ourselves. Teach us to obey You always. Amen.

Friday:

Reading: Ruth 3: 7–12.

Thought: Are we conscious of the needs of our own relations?

Prayer: Lord, show us the needs of those who are related to us, and make us ready and quick to help them. Amen.

Saturday:

Reading: Ruth 3: 12–13.

Thought: Another person's failure is our opportunity, NOT our excuse!

Prayer: O God, help us to meet our responsibilities, not to shirk them, so that the helpless may be helped, the homeless sheltered and the hungry fed. Amen.

Sunday:

Reading: Ruth 3: 14–18.

Thought: Patience is a virtue.

Prayer: O Lord, teach us to sit still and wait for Thee to show us the right path. Amen.

Grace for the Week:

We thank You Lord for this food, and ask Your blessing on all who have laboured in any way that we might be fed. Amen.

Monday:

Reading: Ruth 4: 1–6.

Thought: Money should always be earned.

Prayer: O Lord Who has given us so bounteously the gifts of money, and a home, and a family—make us wary of acquiring wealth the easy way, without earning it or deserving it. Amen.

Tuesday:

Reading: Ruth 4: 8–12.

Thought: Good works are a good witness.

Prayer: Our Father, may all our works be a good witness to You, so that we can be "workmen who are not ashamed". Amen.

Wednesday:

Reading: Ruth 4: 13–17.

Thought: God can bring happiness out of the most hopeless situations.

Prayer: O Lord, give us the kind of faith and trust that believes that all things work together for good to them that love God. Amen.

Thursday:

Reading: Romans 1: 8–12. (It is suggested that these readings should be taken from Phillips' translation.)

Thought: Do we help each other?

Prayer: Dear Lord, help us to help each other, so that our faith in You may grow stronger every day. Amen.

Friday:

Reading: Romans 2: 6–10.

Thought: What will OUR reward be?

Prayer: Dear God, may we remember that one day we shall have to answer to You for all our actions here on earth. Amen.

Saturday:

Reading: Romans 5: 1–5.

Thought: Eternal life begins here.

Prayer: Heavenly Father, when things go wrong and trouble comes, give us Your peace, and use our difficulties to strengthen us in Your service. Amen.

Sunday:

Reading: Romans 5: 6–8.

Thought: If Christ died for us, we should want to live for Him.

Prayer: O Lord, help us to serve Thee as Thou deservest, to give and not to count the cost, to fight and not to heed the wounds, to toil and not to seek for rest, to labour and to ask for no reward, save that of knowing that we do Thy will. Amen.

St. Ignatius Loyola.

Grace for the Week:

At our table every day,
Be Thou with us, Lord, we pray;
Bless the food that we may eat,
Simple fare or party treat;
Make us thankful, Lord, to Thee,
For the good food we can see.

Amen.

Monday:

Reading: Romans 7: 15, 24, 25.

Thought: Do we remember the only way out at times like these?

Prayer: Dear Lord, when good and evil fight together in our lives, give good the victory, through Thy strength, we pray Thee. Amen.

Tuesday:

Reading: Romans 8: 14–17.

Thought: Do we always behave as worthy members of God's family?

Prayer: O God, help us to remember that we are Thy sons and daughters, and may we bring credit upon Thy name. Amen.

Wednesday:

Reading: Romans 8: 28.

Thought: Nothing can happen to us unless God allows it.

Prayer: Father in heaven, remind us that You are always watching over us and that our good is Your concern. Amen.

Thursday:

Reading: Romans 12: 18–21.

Thought: Do we return good for evil?

Prayer: Father in heaven, help us to return good for evil, kind words for harsh ones, and loving actions for unkind ones as You have bidden us. Amen.

Friday:

Reading: Romans 13: 3–7.

Thought: Man's laws are often God-made.

Prayer: O Lord, help us to keep the laws of our country and the rules of our schools, but help us above all to live in obedience to You. Amen.

Saturday:

Reading: Romans 13: 8–10.

Thought: What is the most important commandment?

Prayer: Dear Lord, help us to love each other so that we shall be doing Your will. Amen.

Sunday:

Reading: Romans 13: 11–14.

Thought: Remember that God sees all.

Prayer: Remind us, O Lord, that each day brings Thy second coming nearer, and help us to live completely unto Thee. Amen.

Grace for the Week:

God bless our meal,
God guide our ways,
God give us grace
Our Lord to please.

Monday:

Reading: Romans 14: 1–4.

Thought: We are not ALWAYS right!

Prayer: O Lord, help us to understand that there are many paths that lead to Thee, and that OUR way isn't necessarily the only one. Amen.

Tuesday:

Reading: Romans 14: 10–13.

Thought: Let us keep criticism for ourselves.

Prayer: O God, teach us to make excuses and allowances for other people, and to stop making excuses and allowances for ourselves. Amen.

Wednesday:

Reading: Romans 14: 20, 21.

Thought: Can our actions hinder someone else's faith?

Prayer: Father, give us more concern for our fellow Christians' welfare; and may we never be guilty of leading other people astray. Amen.

Thursday:

Reading: Romans 15: 1–4.

Thought: Have we ever helped anyone to find God?

Prayer: Help us to help other people to find Thee for their own Saviour. Amen.

Friday:

Reading: Romans 16: 17–20.

Thought: Avoid those people who would lead you away from God.

Prayer: O God, Who has been pleased to show us the happiness of living unto Thee: help us to avoid the influence of any who would seek to turn our feet away from Thy paths. Amen.

Saturday:

Reading: Proverbs 2: 1–5.

Thought: Only those who seek, shall find.

Prayer: O God, make us want to seek out Your Words, and to hide Your laws within our hearts. Amen.

Sunday:

Reading: Proverbs 2: 10–15.

Thought: The wise man walks in God's way.

Prayer: O Lord, keep our feet in Your paths, and help us to turn from the crooked ways. Amen.

Grace for the Week:

We thank You Lord for these Your gifts; and ask Your blessing for those who with unfailing courage and faithfulness risk their lives daily to bring them to us. Amen.

Monday:

Reading: Proverbs 30: 7–9.

Thought: We might well echo Solomon's prayer.

Prayer: O God, give us sufficient for our daily needs, and save us from poverty or great riches. Amen.

Tuesday:

Reading: Proverbs 30: 24–28.

Thought: Do we build on the Rock?

Prayer: O God, however feeble we are, teach us the wisdom of building our lives on firm foundations. Amen.

Wednesday:

Reading: Proverbs 31: 10–12.

Thought: Do we "do people good"?

Prayer: O Lord, help us to do people good and not evil, all the days of our life. Amen.

Thursday:

Reading: Proverbs 31: 13–15.

Thought: Do we remember how hard Mother works?

Prayer: O God, we thank You for our Mother. Make us appreciate all that she does for us. Amen.

Friday:

Reading: Proverbs 31: 20–21.

Thought: Are we thankful for warm clothes?

Prayer: O Lord, we give You thanks for the comfort of warm clothes. Make us mindful of those without them. Amen.

Saturday:

Reading: Proverbs 31: 23–27.

Thought: Is our tongue known for its kindness?

Prayer: Gracious Lord, help us to refrain from speaking unkind words, so that our tongue may be known for its kindness. Amen.

Sunday:

Reading: Proverbs 31: 28–31.

Thought: Do our works praise us?

Prayer: Heavenly Father show us that good work, well done, is praise in itself, because it honours You. Amen.

Grace for the Week:

Lord, another day is dawning,
And another meal is spread;
So we bow our heads and humbly
Thank You for our daily bread.
                              Amen.

Monday:

Reading: Genesis 1: 1–5.

Thought: The world would be a dark place without God.

Prayer: We thank You, God, for the sun which lights the world and causes all things living to grow. Amen.

Tuesday:

Reading: Genesis 1: 6–8.

Thought: The sky is everywhere—so is Jesus.

Prayer: Dear Father, as we look at the sky above us, and breathe the air around us, remind us how You are around us and within us all the time. Amen.

Wednesday:

Reading: Genesis 1: 9–13.

Thought: Seeds should grow into healthy plants.

Prayer: Lord Jesus, we ask that the seeds of Your love planted in our hearts may grow bigger and stronger every day. Amen.

Thursday:

Reading: Genesis 1: 14–19.

Thought: There is room for the "greater" and the "less" in God's world.

Prayer: O God, Who has given to each one of us our place and task in the world, help us to do it as well as we can. Amen.

Friday:

Reading: Genesis 1: 20–23.

Thought: Everything fitted into God's plan—do we?

Prayer: O Lord God, help us to fit into Your plans so that we too may deserve Your blessing. Amen.

Saturday:

Reading: Genesis 1: 24–25.

Thought: Do we remember that animals are God's creatures?

Prayer: Bless, we pray You Lord today, all the people who work with sick animals. Help us always to be kind to our pets and to remember their needs. Amen.

Sunday:

Reading: Genesis 1: 26–28.

Thought: Does God see anything of Himself in us?

Prayer: O God, take away all things that make us unlike You, and help us to become more like You, in all that we say and do. Amen.

Grace for the Week:

For food and fellowship, we thank You, Lord. Amen.

Monday:

Reading: Genesis 2: 1–3.

Thought: Do *we* keep holy one day a week?

Prayer: O God, Who at the beginning of the world set aside one day in seven as a special day, help us to keep Your day holy every week. Amen.

Tuesday:

Reading: Genesis: 2: 7–9.

Thought: God knows man's needs—and meets them.

Prayer: O Father God, Who made us and gave us life—we thank You for providing for all our needs in such a wonderful way. Amen.

Wednesday:

Reading: Genesis 2: 15–17.

Thought: Are we obedient to God's commands?

Prayer: O God, Who in Your wisdom knows what is good and what is bad for us. Help us to keep the laws which You have given us. Amen.

Thursday:

Reading: Genesis 2: 18–20.

Thought: God wants us to work *with* Him.

Prayer: O God, Who asked for man's help in naming the creatures of the world—show us how we can share in Your work today, to Your glory. Amen.

Friday:

Reading: Genesis 2: 21–24.

Thought: Christian marriage was God's idea.

Prayer: O God, Who has given to us the happiness and blessing of marriage and the joy of children—may our home be always kept together by Your love. Amen.

Saturday:

Reading: Genesis 3: 1–4.

Thought: Satan always tells untruths.

Prayer: O God, we know that You have made certain laws so that by keeping them we may live in peace and contentment. Make us wary of those who treat Your laws lightly, and would have us do the same. Amen.

Sunday:

Reading: Genesis 3: 5–6.

Thought: Our fall may cause others to stumble.

Prayer: O God, we know that when we fall down through disobedience we often cause someone else to stumble. Help us to remember this, and to keep steadfastly to Your paths. Amen.

Grace for the Week:

Father, give us thankful hearts,
To see this food upon our table,
Remind us of the hungry folk,
And let us help as we are able.
Amen.

Monday:

Reading: Genesis 3: 8–9.

Thought: We can never hide our sin from God.

Prayer: Father, give us courage to seek You when we have done wrong and not to hide from You —because only in seeking forgiveness can we be made clean. Amen.

Tuesday:

Reading: Genesis 3: 12–13.

Thought: Blaming others does not make *us* less guilty.

Prayer: O Lord, we confess that often we do wrong things for which no one is to blame but ourselves. Give us Your forgiveness, we pray You. Amen.

Wednesday:

Reading: Genesis 3: 22–23.

Thought: Man knows good from evil.

Prayer: O God, Who has given to each one of us, however young or small, a knowledge of good and evil—may our own actions never shut us away from Your Presence. Amen.

Thursday:

Reading: Genesis 4: 1–5.

Thought: We mustn't be jealous of the success of others.

Prayer: O Lord God, help us to share in other people's successes and not to be jealous when their work gains more praise than our own. Amen.

Friday:

Reading: Genesis 4: 8–9.

Thought: Jealousy can quickly grow.

Prayer: O Father God, we know that unchecked sins can multiply and grow. Show us our faults and help us to overcome them. Amen.

Saturday:

Reading: Genesis 12: 1–2.

Thought: Obedience brings blessing.

Prayer: O God, when You speak, may we listen. When You send us, teach us to go forth. When You promise, we know You will perform. Amen.

Sunday:

Reading: Genesis 13: 5–7.

Thought: Riches do not bring contentment.

Prayer: O Lord Jesus, Who taught us that happiness is not found in many possessions and Who Yourself possessed nothing —give us the contentment that is found only in You. Amen.

Grace for the Week:

For supplying our needs on this and every day we give You thanks, O Lord. Amen.

Monday:

Reading: Genesis 13: 8–9.

Thought: Are we peacemakers?

Prayer: Lord Jesus, make us peacemakers in all things great and small, so that we forget our own rights and seek only Your glory. Amen.

Tuesday:

Reading: Genesis 13: 10–13.

Thought: Prosperity can bring danger.

Prayer: O Lord, help us to recognize wickedness and evil for what it is, and give us power to turn away. Amen.

Wednesday:

Reading: Genesis 14: 14–16.

Thought: Evil must be fought and conquered.

Prayer: O God, when we see others bound in sin, show us the way in which, with Your help, we can aid them most. Amen.

Thursday:

Reading: Genesis 15: 1.

Thought: God is *our* shield and our reward.

Prayer: Our Father, protect us all the day long, we pray You, and may we find great reward in Your service. Amen.

Friday:

Reading: Genesis 24: 1–4.

Thought: A married couple need to have the same Lord.

Prayer: O Lord, help us to pull together because we serve You, and may our children grow up to love You and one day found other Christian homes. Amen.

Saturday:

Reading: Genesis 24: 10–12.

Thought: Prayer is the key to success.

Prayer: Teach us, O God, the wisdom of praying before we act, so that whatever we do may be in accordance with Your will. Amen.

Sunday:

Reading: Genesis 24: 15–18.

Thought: Kindness is a goodly virtue.

Prayer: Lord Jesus, make us kind to one another, ever willing to serve each other and our fellow men. Amen.

Grace for the Week:

For sun and rain
To swell the grain
To make the bread,
With which we're fed,
We thank You, God. Amen.

Monday:

Reading: Genesis 24: 19–21.

Thought: Rebekah was willing to do *more* than she was asked.

Prayer: O Lord, may we never be weary of serving others, especially when it is to our own inconvenience. Amen.

Tuesday:

Reading: Genesis 24: 22–25.

Thought: Are we hospitable?

Prayer: O Lord, Who has given us a comfortable home in which to live, show us how we can share its benefits with those who may need its shelter. Amen.

Wednesday:

Reading: Genesis 24: 32–33.

Thought: Do we put duty first?

Prayer: O God, make us more ready to work for You than to satisfy our needs, so that others may judge the importance of our message by our concern. Amen.

Thursday:

Reading: Genesis 24: 34–38.

Thought: Are *we* proud of our Master?

Prayer: Dear Lord Jesus, make us proud to be known as Your servants and ever ready to speak of Your greatness. Amen.

Friday:

Reading: Genesis 24: 42–44.

Thought: Would we have passed the servant's "test"?

Prayer: O Father God, we never know who is watching us, or listening to us as we go about our daily work. Remind us that other people judge our worth as Christians by what we do and say. Amen.

Saturday:

Reading: Genesis 24: 45–47.

Thought: God's answers sometimes come more quickly than we expect.

Prayer: O God, when You answer our prayers "before we have finished praying", and sometimes give us things before we ask at all, remind us to thank You for providing for our needs. Amen.

Sunday:

Reading: Genesis 24: 50–53.

Thought: How quickly do we recognize God's hand at work?

Prayer: God our Father, give us eyes that are quick to recognize when plans proceed from You, and make us prompt to carry them through. Amen.

Grace for the Week:

We thank You, Lord, for this food, and for the hands that have prepared it. Amen.

Monday:

Reading: Genesis 24: 55–56.

Thought: Never put off until tomorrow what should be done today!

Prayer: O Lord Jesus, we confess to You how often we "put off" until a more convenient time, tasks that should be done today. Help us to overcome this fault, we pray You. Amen.

Tuesday:

Reading: Genesis 24: 61–63.

Thought: Prayer prepares.

Prayer: O God, may we be ready to face all great changes in our lives because we have prepared ourselves in quietly talking with You. Amen.

Wednesday:

Reading: Genesis 24: 64–67.

Thought: We, too, have a Comforter in times of sorrow.

Prayer: Lord Jesus, Who sent Your Holy Spirit to be our Comforter in times of grief, be near to all those who need You today. Amen.

Thursday:

Reading: Genesis 26: 19–22.

Thought: How often do *we* "give in"?

Prayer: Lord God Almighty, help us to be prepared to "give in" to other people, if by doing so we can avoid a quarrel. Amen.

Friday:

Reading: Genesis 26: 23–25.

Thought: Sometimes we need reminding of God's presence.

Prayer: O gracious God, keep us ever mindful of Your presence with us, so that we may never need to fear anything in life. Amen.

Saturday:

Reading: Genesis 26: 26–29.

Thought: Do others see that the Lord is with us?

Prayer: O Lord Jesus, others will want to serve You if our lives show them Your presence, In all that we say and do today may we honour You. Amen.

Sunday:

Reading: Genesis 27: 1–4.

Thought: Old people are very dependent on young ones.

Prayer: Give us a love for old people, O Lord, and make us quick to see their needs and ever ready to help them. Amen.

Grace for the Week:

Morning is here
The table is spread,
Thanks be to God
Who gives us bread. Amen.

Monday:

Reading: Genesis 27: 5–10.

Thought: It is dangerous to have "favourites".

Prayer: O Lord Jesus, give each one of us an equal love for the other, and give to all of us an over-ruling love for You. Amen.

Tuesday:

Reading: Genesis 27: 11–14.

Thought: It is wicked to use our influence wrongly.

Prayer: O God, may we never use our influence to persuade someone else to do wrong, because in doing so we are really guilty of their sin. Amen.

Wednesday:

Reading: Genesis 27: 15–19.

Thought: Lies and deceit cannot lead to true blessing.

Prayer: O heavenly Father, cleanse our lips so that You can speak through them, and give us, we pray You, Your blessing. Amen.

Thursday:

Reading: Genesis 27: 20–22.

Thought: One lie leads to another.

Prayer: O Lord Jesus, keep us from the habit of lying, we beseech You, because we know that it is a habit that is very hard to break. Amen.

Friday:

Reading: Genesis 27: 34–35.

Thought: Wrongs cannot always be righted.

Prayer: O God, we know that sometimes our actions lead to wrongdoing that cannot be put right. Keep us in mind of this, so that we think before we act. Amen.

Saturday:

Reading: Genesis 27: 41–44.

Thought: A mother can sow hate between her children.

Prayer: O Lord Jesus, fill the mother of this family with so much love that it may overflow to everyone in it, so that love may abound in this home. Amen.

Sunday:

Reading: Genesis 33: 1–4.

Thought: It takes a great heart to forgive.

Prayer: O Lord Jesus, teach us how to forgive others as You have forgiven us, for in cherishing resentment we only make ourselves unhappy. Amen.

Grace for the Week:

Dear Lord, accept our grateful thanks for this food, which will strengthen our bodies to serve You. Amen.

Monday:

Reading: 1 Corinthians 1: 26–29.

Thought: God chooses and uses us.

Prayer: O God, we thank You that we do not have to be wise or important to be chosen by You. Use us as we are, we pray You. Amen.

Tuesday:

Reading: 1 Corinthians 3: 1–3.

Thought: Is there jealousy and squabbling among us?

Prayer: O Lord Jesus, we confess that sometimes jealousy and squabbling spoils our love for each other and for You. Forgive us this wrongdoing and help us to overcome it. Amen.

Wednesday:

Reading: 1 Corinthians 3: 9–11.

Thought: Foundations are important.

Prayer: O God, remind us that each day we are adding to the building of our lives. Help us to build on firm foundations and to Your Glory. Amen.

Thursday:

Reading: 1 Corinthians 3: 16–19(a).

Thought: Do we treat our bodies as God's Temple?

Prayer: O Lord Jesus, Who lives within us, and speaks through us, keep our bodies and minds clean and wholesome so that we are a fit home for Your Spirit. Amen.

Friday:

Reading: 1 Corinthians 4: 1–4.

Thought: Do we know our own faults?

Prayer: Show us what we are really like, O Lord, so that we may be saved from becoming self-satisfied. Amen.

Saturday:

Reading: 1 Corinthians 4: 5.

Thought: What are our reasons for doing good?

Prayer: O Lord, help us to do good and kindly deeds for Your praise alone, and not for the praise of men. Amen.

Sunday:

Reading: 1 Corinthians 4: 9–12.

Thought: How do we behave in unfavourable circumstances?

Prayer: Lord Jesus, when things are against us, be Thou for us, so that we may always be able to show to others Thy wonderful example of patience. Amen.

Grace for the Week:

Thou art the bread of life,
Upon Thy Word we feed,
We thank Thee too for daily food
To meet our every need. Amen.

Monday:

Reading: 1 Corinthians 10: 12-13.

Thought: Temptation is a bridge, not a wall.

Prayer: O God, when we are tempted to do wrong remind us that we can trust You to help us if we only remember to turn to You. Amen.

Tuesday:

Reading: 1 Corinthians 12: 14-17.

Thought: Where does our usefulness lie?

Prayer: O Lord, show us our job within Your Church, and help us to do it with all our might. Amen.

Wednesday:

Reading: 1 Corinthians 12:18-22.

Thought: There are no surplus Christians.

Prayer: Dear Father God, we know You can use even the most feeble amongst us in Your Service. Show us that we are necessary in the important task of spreading Your Kingdom. Amen.

Thursday:

Reading: 1 Corinthians 13: 1-3.

Thought: God's values are different from man's.

Prayer: Our Father, sometimes we think that by doing great works we are serving You best. Teach us how wrong we are. Amen.

Friday:

Reading: 1 Corinthians 13: 4-7.

Thought: Most of our love is not worthy of the name.

Prayer: Lord Jesus, please teach us how to love unselfishly, without possessiveness and without limits. Amen.

Saturday:

Reading: 1 Corinthians 15: 58.

Thought: Nothing we do for God is "in vain".

Prayer: O God, You know that we sometimes feel that the tasks we do are so humble that they hardly count. Remind us that nothing is in vain that we do in Your Name. Amen.

Sunday:

Reading: 1 Corinthians 16: 1-2.

Thought: Giving should be organized.

Prayer: O Lord, help us to consider carefully how You have prospered us, so that Your work may not suffer for lack of funds. Amen.

Grace for the Week:

We give You thanks, Our Father, for providing this food to meet our daily needs. Amen.

Monday:

Reading: Jonah 1: 1–3.

Thought: Do we turn a "deaf ear" to God's commands?

Prayer: O God, we confess how often our wishes clash with Your commands. Help us not to run away from the tasks which You have set us. Amen.

Tuesday:

Reading: Jonah 1: 4–5.

Thought: Are we sometimes unconscious of having caused a storm?

Prayer: O Lord, show us when we have been the cause of a "storm" in our home, our church or our school, and give us grace to dispel it. Amen.

Wednesday:

Reading: Jonah 1: 11, 12, 15.

Thought: Jonah took his punishment, Jesus took ours.

Prayer: O Lord Jesus Christ, Who bore the punishment for our sins, make us mindful of Your sacrifice and willing to accept it. Amen.

Thursday:

Reading: Jonah 1: 16–17 and Jonah 2: 1.

Thought: God hears prayer from anywhere.

Prayer: O heavenly Father, we thank You for the knowledge that we can pray to You at any time and in any place. Teach us how to "pray without ceasing". Amen.

Friday:

Reading: Jonah 2: 10 and Jonah 3: 1–3.

Thought: God often gives us a second chance.

Prayer: O Father God, we admit that we often fail You. Give us a second chance to obey Your voice. Amen.

Saturday:

Reading: Jonah 3: 4, 5, 10.

Thought: God longs to see repentánce.

Prayer: O God, we know that You want us to be really sorry for our wrongdoings so that You can forgive us. Soften our hearts and help us to ask Your forgiveness. Amen.

Sunday:

Reading: Jonah 4: 1, 2.

Thought: Do we dare to be less forgiving than God?

Prayer: O God, we confess with shame that we sometimes feel that certain people do not deserve Your forgiveness. Give us the strength to pray wholeheartedly for those we love the least. Amen.

Grace for the Week:

Blessed Lord, we pray Thee to be
present at our table,
Hallowing Thy gifts to our use,
That eating to satisfy our needs
We may remember those who lack.
                    Amen.

Monday:

Reading: Colossians 1: 1–4.

Thought: Do we write to, and pray for, our friends?

Prayer: O Lord, remind us today of those friends to whom we should write, and for whom we should pray.   Amen.

Tuesday:

Reading: Colossians 1: 5–6.

Thought: Is our faith bringing forth fruit?

Prayer: Lord Jesus, may our faith not be like a barren tree, which has nothing to show, but as a fruitful tree full of grace and truth.   Amen.

Wednesday:

Reading: Colossians 1: 7–9.

Thought: Do we know God's will for us?

Prayer: Gracious Lord, fill us with the knowledge of Your will for us in our daily lives.   Amen.

Thursday:

Reading: Colossians 1: 10–13.

Thought: Is our work "pleasing" to God?

Prayer: Lord Jesus Christ, help us to walk worthily of You, being fruitful in every good work and increasing in the knowledge of God.   Amen.

Friday:

Reading: Colossians 2: 6–7.

Thought: How firmly are we rooted in the faith?

Prayer: O God, help us to stand firm always in the Christian faith, whatever life may bring. Amen.

Saturday:

Reading: Colossians 3: 1–2.

Thought: Where is our affection set?

Prayer: O Lord Jesus, set our affection on lasting things of value that will never pass away. Amen.

Sunday:

Reading: Colossians 3: 12–14.

Thought: Are these *our* virtues?

Prayer: Lord Jesus, give us the gifts of mercy, kindness, humility, and long suffering, so that we may follow in Your footsteps.   Amen.

Grace for the Week:

Great God, Thou Giver of all
good,
Accept our praise and bless our
food.
Grace, health and strength to us
afford,
Through Jesus Christ, our Risen
Lord.   *Amen.*

Monday:

Reading: Colossians 3: 16–17.

Thought: Do we do every-
thing as if it is for the Lord?

Prayer: May everything we do
today, be done as if it were for
the Lord Jesus.   Amen.

Tuesday:

Reading: Colossians 3: 18–21.

Thought: God's recipe for a
happy family.

Prayer: O God, make our
family a truly happy one because
each member seeks to serve and
obey You.   Amen.

Wednesday:

Reading: Colossians 3: 22–25.

Thought: God's recipe for a
contented wage-earner.

Prayer: Lord Jesus, if we belong to You, then You are our
true employer. Help us to remember this in all that we do. Amen.

Thursday:

Reading: Colossians 4: 5–6.

Thought: Do we make the best
possible use of our time?

Prayer: Heavenly Father, You
have given to each of us twenty-
four hours each day. Help us to
make the best possible use of our
time and not to waste it.   Amen.

Friday:

Reading: 2 Timothy 2: 20–21.

Thought: Are we ready
vessels?

Prayer: O Lord, make us clean
and serviceable vessels, ready for
our Master's use.   Amen.

Saturday:

Reading: 2 Timothy 3: 14–15.

Thought: Are our minds open
to God's teaching?

Prayer: Dear God, as each day
we read Your Word, open our
minds to the teaching within it.
Amen.

Sunday:

Reading: 2 Timothy 4: 16–18.

Thought: God is our most
reliable Defender.

Prayer: O God, help us to
remember that You will stand
by us, when all others may fail
us.   Amen.

Grace for the Week:

For health and strength and daily food,
We praise Thy Name, O Lord.

Monday:

Reading: Joshua 1: 1–3.

Thought: No one is indispensable.

Prayer: Dear Lord, save us from self-importance, and help us to realize that Your work must go on even if we are set aside. Amen.

Tuesday:

Reading: Joshua 1: 7–8.

Thought: God's Word is OUR strength.

Prayer: O Lord, make us strong and brave to obey Your Word as you speak to us through it each day. Amen.

Wednesday:

Reading: Judges 6: 11–14.

Thought: God sees what we CAN be, as well as what we ARE.

Prayer: O God, make us able to become mighty men and women and boys and girls of valour in Thy Service. Amen.

Thursday:

Reading: Judges 6: 15–16.

Thought: Everyone has a part in God's plans.

Prayer: Lord Jesus, please show us what You would have us do for You, and give us the strength to do it. Amen.

Friday:

Reading: Judges 7: 2–3.

Thought: Less of self and more of Thee.

Prayer: Dear Lord, help us to be less ready to praise ourselves and more ready to praise You in everything we say and do. Amen.

Saturday:

Reading: Judges 7: 4–6.

Thought: Are we alert?

Prayer: O God, keep us from being so concerned with our daily round that we forget to be alert and watchful for temptations. Amen.

Sunday:

Reading: Judges 7: 7–8.

Thought: Victories are not always won by numbers.

Prayer: O God, teach us how strong we are when You are with us, and how weak when we stand alone. Amen.

Grace for the Week:

We give Thee thanks, O Father,
For all Thy gifts of food;
O give us thankful, praising hearts,
And make us kind and good.
Amen.

Monday:

Reading: Judges 7: 16–18.

Thought: Would *we* dare to say: "Look on me and do likewise?"

Prayer: O Lord Jesus, You are our only pattern and example. May we "look on You, and do likewise". Amen.

Tuesday:

Reading: Judges 7: 19–21.

Thought: Obedience brings victory.

Prayer: O God, teach us to obey every whisper of Your voice, so that we may have victory over sin and temptation. Amen.

Wednesday:

Reading: Judges 8: 22–23.

Thought: Remember that God is our King and Ruler.

Prayer: O heavenly Father, be our King, rule over us in everything. Amen.

Thursday:

Reading: 1 Timothy 1: 12–15.

(It is suggested that these readings should be taken from J. B. Phillips' translation.)

Thought: No one is too bad for God to use.

Prayer: O God, show us our faults, so that we may ask You for forgiveness. Amen.

Friday:

Reading: 1 Timothy 6: 7–10.

Thought: Money should be a servant, not a master.

Prayer: O Lord, help us to use in the right way the money and position that You have given us. Amen.

Saturday:

Reading: 1 Timothy 6: 11–14.

Thought: It is not always cowardly to run away!

Prayer: Dear Father God, show us those things we should avoid, and teach us those things that we should seek. Amen.

Sunday:

Reading: 1 Timothy 6: 17–19.

Thought: Eternal treasure will never lose its value.

Prayer: O Lord, help us to lay up for ourselves treasure in heaven which will be of everlasting value. Amen.

Grace for the Week:

*For the farmers who have worked
    that we may eat,
For those who have bought and sold
    this food,
For those who have prepared it,
And most of all for You who
    planned it,
We thank You, God.   Amen.*

Monday:

Reading: James 2: 1–5.

Thought: Are we "snobs"?

Prayer: Lord Jesus Christ, help us to judge a person's worth by his faith in You, and not by his earthly riches. Amen.

Tuesday:

Reading: James 2: 14–17.

Thought: Have we faith *and* works?

Prayer: O Merciful Father, Who meets our daily needs so faithfully, make us conscious of the needs of those less fortunate than ourselves.   Amen.

Wednesday:

Reading: James 3: 7–10.

Thought: Is our tongue "tamed"?

Prayer: O God, help us today to tame our tongues, so that the words we speak are those of kindness, politeness and love.   Amen.

Thursday:

Reading: James 4: 7–10.

Thought: Does sin make us "deeply sorry"?

Prayer: Loving Father, as we draw near to You just now, make us deeply sorry for anything that we have done wrong, and forgive us, we pray You.   Amen.

Friday:

Reading: James 4: 11–12.

Thought: Do we judge others?

Prayer: O God, help us to keep our lips from speaking unkindly about other people and make us slow to judge their actions.   Amen.

Saturday:

Reading: James 4: 13–16.

Thought: Man proposes—God disposes.

Prayer: Our Father God, teach us to lay our plans before You, for Your approval, so that we may know that we are doing Your will.   Amen.

Sunday:

Reading: James 5: 19–20.

Thought: Are we on the lookout for those who have wandered?

Prayer: Lord Jesus, Who came to seek and save the lost, give us Your followers a love and concern for those who have wandered away from You.   Amen.

Grace for the Week:

For sweet milk and pure water,
For crisp cereals and brown eggs,
For fresh bread and creamy butter,
We thank You, dear Father.
                              Amen.

Monday:

Reading: Esther 1: 1–4.

Thought: Do we like to "show off" our possessions?

Prayer: Dear Father God, help us to look upon our possessions as gifts from You, and not as symbols of our own importance. Amen.

Tuesday:

Reading: Esther 1: 5–6.

Thought: Do we live in unnecessary luxury?

Prayer: Dear Lord Jesus, help us to plan our spending with prayer, so that we do not forget our starving brothers in other lands. Amen.

Wednesday:

Reading: Esther 1: 7–9.

Thought: We, too, are free to choose.

Prayer: Dear God, Who has given to us a free choice between right and wrong, give us wisdom to choose the right way in all things. Amen.

Thursday:

Reading: Esther 1: 10–12.

Thought: Do we refuse to do the wrong thing?

Prayer: Heavenly Father, give us courage to say "no" when other people try to persuade us to do what we know to be wrong. Amen.

Friday:

Reading: Esther 1: 13–15.

Thought: God's advice is wiser than man's.

Prayer: Gracious Father, teach us to turn to You in all our doubts, and guide our thoughts and actions, we pray You. Amen.

Saturday:

Reading: Esther 1: 16–17.

Thought: Are we harsh in our judgment of others?

Prayer: Dear God, give us love in viewing the actions of others, because we know we are dependent on Your love for our own forgiveness. Amen.

Sunday:

Reading: Esther 1: 18–20.

Thought: God does not judge as man judges.

Prayer: Heavenly Father, we thank You that You do not judge us upon outward appearances, but on the attitude of our inmost hearts. Amen.

Grace for the Week:

At breakfast, dinner-time and tea,
Our grateful thanks we raise to
Thee,
Who sees the meanest sparrow fall,
And grants His blessing to us all.
                    Amen.

Monday:

Reading: Esther 1: 21–22.

Thought: Important letters shouldn't be written in haste.

Prayer: Dear God, help us to think and pray before we write words that may have a lasting effect upon others. Amen.

Tuesday:

Reading: Esther 2: 1–4.

Thought: Even important people can be easily replaced.

Prayer: Dear Lord, we are sometimes tempted to think we are indispensable. Remind us how easily we can be replaced. Amen.

Wednesday:

Reading: Esther 2: 5–7.

Thought: Do we care for the orphaned?

Prayer: Father in heaven, thank you for those who spend their lives caring for fatherless and motherless children. Show us any way in which we can help their work. Amen.

Thursday:

Reading: Esther 2: 8–9.

Thought: Do other people like us?

Prayer: Dear Lord Jesus, help us to be the kind of people who inspire liking in our fellow men. Amen.

Friday:

Reading: Esther 2: 10–11.

Thought: Do we care "what becomes of" our relations?

Prayer: Dear Father, Who in Your love has set us in a family: give us a real love and concern for the well-being of one another. Amen.

Saturday:

Reading: Esther 2: 15–17.

Thought: It is difficult to fill leading positions satisfactorily.

Prayer: Our heavenly King, when You put us in a position of responsibility, help us to fill it with wisdom and grace. Amen.

Sunday:

Reading: Esther 2: 18–20.

Thought: Even queens have to learn obedience!

Prayer: Our heavenly Father, make us obedient to those who are wiser than we are, for we know that all Your servants must learn discipline. Amen.

Grace for the Week:

We thank You once again, dear Lord, for unfailingly supplying our daily needs. May we never take Your provision for granted. Amen.

Monday:

Reading: Esther 3: 1–2.

Thought: Does promotion improve us?

Prayer: Dear God, give us a modest opinion of ourselves, so that we do not seek to set ourselves above our fellow men. Amen.

Tuesday:

Reading: Esther 3: 3–6.

Thought: Are we troublemakers?

Prayer: O Lord, we have to confess how often we make trouble and interfere with things that do not concern us. Forgive us, we pray You. Amen.

Wednesday:

Reading: Esther 3: 8–9.

Thought: Are we determined to get our own way?

Prayer: Dear God, we are ashamed to think how much effort and money we are often prepared to spend so that we can gain our own way. Give us equal keenness to see Your purposes fulfilled. Amen.

Thursday:

Reading: Esther 3: 10–11 and 13.

Thought: The results of evil are far-reaching.

Prayer: Our heavenly King, we can see from Your Book how one evil man can cause endless sadness. Cleanse us from our sin, Lord, so that You can use us for good. Amen.

Friday:

Reading: Esther 4: 1–3.

Thought: *Our* King's commandments bring happiness.

Prayer: Dear heavenly King, we thank You because we know that obeying Your commandments brings us peace and happiness. Be with those who live under a rule of fear. Amen.

Saturday:

Reading: Esther 4: 5–8.

Thought: Do we seek the cause of other people's unhappiness?

Prayer: Dear God, give us a real concern for the unhappiness of others, and help us to relieve their sorrow when we can. Amen.

Sunday:

Reading: Esther 4: 9–12.

Thought: Difficulties have to be overcome.

Prayer: Almighty God, to whom no difficulties are insurmountable, give Your people the courage to trust in Your strength. Amen.

Grace for the Week:

*God Who made the flowers and
trees
And sends the sun and rain,
Gives to us our food, for which
We thank Him once again.*
                              Amen.

Monday:

Reading: Esther 4: 13-14.

Thought: Do we take, or lose, our greatest opportunities?

Prayer: Dear Lord, Who has set us in our different places to further Your purposes. Help us to fulfil Your plans.   Amen.

Tuesday:

Reading: Esther 4: 15-17.

Thought: Do we plan our actions carefully?

Prayer: O Lord, show us the wisdom of planning ahead before we tackle an important piece of work for You.   Amen.

Wednesday:

Reading: Esther 5: 1-4.

Thought: God can smooth our paths.

Prayer: Dear God, smooth our paths so that we may speak and work for You without hindrance, we pray You.   Amen.

Thursday:

Reading: Esther 7: 1-4.

Thought: God can give us the right words to speak.

Prayer: O heavenly King, put the words into our mouths, so that we may speak with wisdom when we are called upon to do so.   Amen.

Friday:

Reading: Esther 7: 5-7 and 10.

Thought: Sin deserves punishment.

Prayer: Dear Lord Jesus, Who died to take the punishment for our sin: remind us of our debt of love to You.   Amen.

Saturday:

Reading: Esther 8: 3-5.

Thought: Do we plead with tears to our King?

Prayer: Our gracious King, we plead today for those we love. Bring them to know You as their Saviour, so that they may have everlasting life.   Amen.

Sunday:

Reading: Esther 8: 7-8 and 11.

Thought: God defends us against our enemies.

Prayer: O God our Sure Defender, be our strong shield against our enemies so that they may be powerless to harm us. Amen.

Grace for the Week:

Remind us, dear Lord, to eat of this food gratefully remembering the needy people of other lands. Amen.

Monday:

Reading: Esther 8: 15–17.

Thought: God's care of us should recommend OUR faith.

Prayer: Dear God, Who can frustrate the evil purposes of our enemies so that good may come: May others see Your care of us, and long to shelter under Your protecting love. Amen.

Tuesday:

Reading: 1 Thessalonians 1: 1–3.

Thought: Does our love mean hard work?

Prayer: Lord Jesus Christ, show us that to believe in You means to work for You, and give us joy in our work. Amen.

Wednesday:

Reading: 1 Thessalonians 1: 4–8.

Thought: Are we a "sounding board"?

Prayer: Dear Lord, use us to spread the Word of God so that our faith in You may be made known. Amen.

Thursday:

Reading: 1 Thessalonians 1: 9–10.

Thought: Do we look forward to the Second Coming of the Lord Jesus?

Prayer: Dear Lord Jesus, help us to show in our lives that we are eagerly waiting and watching for Your Second Coming from Heaven. Amen.

Friday:

Reading: 1 Thessalonians 2: 3–6.

Thought: What are our motives for spreading the Gospel?

Prayer: Dear God, You have entrusted us with Your Good News to men: help us to have the right reasons for wanting to bring other people into Your Kingdom. Amen.

Saturday:

Reading: 1 Thessalonians 2: 7–11.

Thought: Do we expect "payment" for preaching the Gospel?

Prayer: Dear Father God, help us to serve You untiringly day and night, without hope of reward, and give us instruction so that we may pass it on to others. Amen.

Sunday:

Reading: 1 Thessalonians 2: 12–13.

Thought: Do we find God's Word a power in our lives?

Prayer: Almighty God, thank You for showing us, day by day, the Power and Truth of Your Word, and help us to use it for the strengthening of our daily lives. Amen.

Grace for the Week:

Give us this day our daily bread,
For by Thy Grace we all are fed.
Amen.

Monday:

Reading: Matthew 19: 13–15.
Thought: Adults can learn from a child's faith.
Prayer: Dear Lord Jesus, give us a simple trust in You, and bless us, we pray You. Amen.

Tuesday:

Reading: Matthew 20: 1–4.
Thought: There is work for everyone in God's vineyard.
Prayer: Dear God, give us the will to work for You so that we may not be guilty of idling our lives away. Amen.

Wednesday:

Reading: Matthew 20: 5–7.
Thought: Have we been "hired" by God?
Prayer: Dear Master, we pray today for those who have not been "hired" to serve You. Call them to Your service, we pray You. Amen.

Thursday:

Reading: Matthew 20: 8–12.
Thought: Do we try to teach God His business?
Prayer: O Lord, forgive us for the times when we argue with Your decisions, and teach us to bow silently and humbly to Your Will. Amen.

Friday:

Reading: Matthew 20: 13–16.
Thought: Have we been called and chosen?
Prayer: Dear Heavenly Father, You have called us to Your service. Make us worthy of our calling through Jesus Christ our Lord. Amen.

Saturday:

Reading: Matthew 21: 1–3.
Thought: Do we lend our possessions to Jesus?
Prayer: Dear Lord Jesus, take our possessions and use them, and us, in Your service. Amen.

Sunday:

Reading: Matthew 21: 6–9.
Thought: Do we follow the crowd?
Prayer: Dear God, help us to have a personal trust in You, that will not be swayed by the actions and words of other people. Amen.

Grace for the Week:

May we who have plenty, remember those who have not, and may we waste nothing that is good to eat and comes from Thy Hand, O God. Amen.

Monday:

Reading: Matthew 21: 10–13.

Thought: Do we use God's House for the right purpose?

Prayer: Dear God, help us to remember that Your House is a house of prayer, and to treat it as such. Amen.

Tuesday:

Reading: Matthew 21: 28–31.

Thought: Which son do we resemble?

Prayer: Lord, make us sorry for the times we fail to obey Your Voice, and help us to show our sorrow by our future behaviour. Amen.

Wednesday:

Reading: Matthew 22: 1–3.

Thought: Do we refuse Christ's invitation?

Prayer: Dear Lord Jesus, we pray today for all those who have heard Your invitation and refused it. Soften their hearts, we pray You. Amen.

Thursday:

Reading: Matthew 22: 4–6.

Thought: Do we treat Christ's invitation lightly?

Prayer: Dear Lord, sometimes we do not realize how much You have done for us. May we never be guilty of treating Your sacrifice lightly. Amen.

Friday:

Reading: Matthew 22: 7–10.

Thought: Will we be at the wedding feast?

Prayer: Dear Lord, we know we are not worthy to be present at Your feast but we thank You for Your love in inviting us, and making it possible for us to attend. Amen.

Saturday:

Reading: Matthew 22: 11–14.

Thought: Will we be correctly dressed?

Prayer: Dear Lord Jesus, please wash our sins away so that our hearts may be clean when we meet You face to face. Amen.

Sunday:

Reading: Revelation 22: 12–14.

Thought: Have we a right to the Tree of Life?

Prayer: Dear Lord Jesus, keep us watchful for Your Coming and faithful to Your commandments, so that one day we may enter through the gates of Your eternal city. Amen.

Grace for the Week:

*To God who gives our daily
 bread
A thankful song we raise
And pray that He who sends us
 food
May fill our hearts with praise.
 Amen.*

Monday:
Reading: Nehemiah 1: 1–4.
 Thought: Does bad news bring *us* to our knees?
 Prayer: O God, give us a love and concern for Christian people in other places, so that we may pray earnestly for their needs. Amen.

Tuesday:
Reading: Nehemiah 2: 1–3.
 Thought: How do we feel when we see God's House neglected?
 Prayer: O God, give us a burden of prayer for the neglect of Your House and the lack of love of Your people, and show us anything we can do to help. Amen.

Wednesday:
Reading: Nehemiah 2: 4–6.
 Thought: Do we make "quick" prayers for guidance?
 Prayer: Heavenly Father, teach us to turn to You for guidance as naturally as we speak to our earthly friends. Amen.

Thursday:
Reading: Nehemiah 2: 7–8.
 Thought: Are we bold to ask for help for God's work?
 Prayer: O Lord God, make us bold in asking for help for the needs of Your Kingdom. Amen.

Friday:
Reading: Nehemiah 2: 11–13.
 Thought: Everyone needs quiet times.
 Prayer: O God, show us the need to be quiet and alone so that we can think of the best way to set about Your work. Amen.

Saturday:
Reading: Nehemiah 2: 14–16.
 Thought: Silence is golden.
 Prayer: O God, teach us that there are times when it is best to keep our thoughts and plans hidden within our hearts. Amen.

Sunday:
Reading: Nehemiah 2: 17–18.
 Thought: Are we ready workers?
 Prayer: God our Father, help us to rise up and build Your Kingdom, and strengthen our hands for this good work. Amen.

Grace for the Week:

We ask You, O Lord, to provide for the needs of others, and give us thankful hearts. Amen.

Monday:

Reading: Nehemiah 2: 19–20.

Thought: There is no place for mockers in God's Kingdom.

Prayer: Almighty God, remind us today that there is no place in Your Kingdom for those who mock and scorn Your Word. Amen.

Tuesday:

Reading: Nehemiah 3: 1 and 4–5.

Thought: Do we put our backs into our work?

Prayer: O God, Who records in Heaven all the work we do for You, help us to serve You with all our might. Amen.

Wednesday:

Reading: Nehemiah 4: 1–3.

Thought: We shouldn't despise the work of others.

Prayer: Lord God, we ask You to keep us from criticizing the work of others while our own hands are idle. Amen.

Thursday:

Reading: Nehemiah 4: 6–8.

Thought: Do we give the Devil cause to be angry?

Prayer: Heavenly Father, give us a mind to work, so that the strengthening of Your Kingdom may give the Devil a cause to be angry. Amen.

Friday:

Reading: Nehemiah 4: 9–11.

Thought: Do we pray AND set a guard?

Prayer: Dear God, teach us to pray, and then do all in our power to prevent the Enemy doing damage to Your work. Amen.

Saturday:

Reading: Nehemiah 4: 12–14.

Thought: Watchfulness guards against defeat.

Prayer: Set a guard over our mouths, O Lord, and keep watch over the door of our lips. Amen.

Sunday:

Reading: Nehemiah 4: 15–16.

Thought: It is sometimes good for leaders to "stand behind".

Prayer: O God, we so often like the highest place and the front rank. Teach us that we can often serve You best by "standing behind". Amen.

Grace for the Week:

Father high in heaven
All by Thee are fed,
Hear Thy children praise Thee
For their daily bread. Amen.

Monday:

Reading: Nehemiah 4: 18–20.
Thought: Unity is strength.
Prayer: We pray today, O Lord, for the unity of Your church, so that with You at our head we may form a strong and solid body against the enemy. Amen.

Tuesday:

Reading: Nehemiah 4: 21–23.
Thought: Christians are "on duty" twenty-four hours a day.
Prayer: O God our Father, remind us that there is no time when we cease to be "on duty" as members of Your family. Amen.

Wednesday:

Reading: Nehemiah 6: 1–3.
Thought: Do we leave jobs unfinished?
Prayer: O God, we know we are doing a great work for You as we seek to spread Your Kingdom on earth. Let us not cease until it is finished. Amen.

Thursday:

Reading: Nehemiah 6: 4–7.
Thought: Self-centred people are puzzled by selfless actions.
Prayer: May all that we do for You, O Lord, be done with no desire for reward or advancement. Amen.

Friday:

Reading: Nehemiah 6: 8–9.
Thought: God strengthens weak hands.
Prayer: When others seek to hinder Your work by weakening our hands, give us of Your strength, we pray You, Lord. Amen.

Saturday:

Reading: Nehemiah 6: 15–16.
Thought: Is our work accomplished with the help of God?
Prayer: O God our Father, let us not forget that all we accomplish in this life is accomplished with Your help. Amen.

Sunday:

Reading: Nehemiah 8: 1–3.
Thought: Are we attentive to God's laws?
Prayer: O Lord, give us ears that listen to the Book of Your law, and hearts that obey it. Amen.

Grace for the Week:

Food, and drink, and shelter,
Warm clothes and cosy beds,
We think of those and thank You
As now we bow our heads. Amen.

Monday:

Reading: Psalm 23: 1–3.

Thought: Do we follow our Leader?

Prayer: O Lord, help us to follow in Your footsteps wherever You may lead. Amen.

Tuesday:

Reading: Psalm 23: 4–6.

Thought: Will we always be found in God's House?

Prayer: O God, give us a love for Your House and grant that we may always be found within it on Your day. Amen.

Wednesday:

Reading: Isaiah 9: 6.

Thought: God's Christmas plans were laid well ahead.

Prayer: Mighty God, our Everlasting Father, help us to look forward to the birthday of the Prince of Peace with expectant hearts. Amen.

Thursday:

Reading: Luke 1: 5–7.

Thought: Are we "truly religious people?"

Prayer: Dear God, help us to keep all Your commandment and requirements so that through the Lord Jesus Christ we may be blameless in Your sight. Amen

Friday:

Reading: Luke 1: 8–12.

Thought: Can our ministe rely on our prayers?

Prayer: Dear Lord Jesus, teach us to pray, so that our ministe may know he can rely on ou prayers as he goes about hi duties among us. Amen.

Saturday:

Reading: Luke 1: 13–17.

Thought: Are we fully read for our Lord?

Prayer: Dear Lord, You hav promised that one day You wil return to this earth. Make us full ready for Your coming. Amen

Sunday:

Reading: Luke 1: 18–20.

Thought: God's word alway comes true at the proper time.

Prayer: Dear God, we confes that often we are impatient whe our prayers are not answere quickly. Remind us of the trut of Gabriel's words. Amen.

Grace for the Week:

We thank You, Lord, for all the joys of Christmastide, and for this food which You have supplied to meet our needs. Amen.

Monday:

Reading: Luke 1: 21–25.

Thought: Do we thank God for answered prayer?

Prayer: Heavenly Father, forgive us for the times when we forget to thank You for answered prayers, and give us more thankful hearts. Amen.

Tuesday:

Reading: Luke 1: 26–28.

Thought: Are we "favoured of God"?

Prayer: Dear God, those people whom You can use are indeed favoured. Make us useful in Your service, we pray You. Amen.

Wednesday:

Reading: Luke 1: 29–33.

Thought: God loves us dearly.

Prayer: God our Father, help us not to be afraid, whatever may happen to us, and remind us that You love us dearly. Amen.

Thursday:

Reading: Luke 1: 34–37.

Thought: God's promises are always fulfilled.

Prayer: Dear God, as we see the fulfilment of Your promises in the Bible and in our daily lives, use this to strengthen our faith, we pray you. Amen.

Friday:

Reading: Luke 1: 38–40.

Thought: Do we belong to the Lord?

Prayer: Dear Lord, we want to belong to You body and soul. Take us, and use us, we pray You. Amen.

Saturday:

Reading: Luke 1: 46–49.

Thought: Does God's service bring a song to our hearts?

Prayer: God our Father, fill our hearts with joy and our mouths with praise, because You have given us the chance to serve You. Amen.

Sunday:

Reading: Luke 1: 56–58.

Thought: Do we share in the joys of others?

Prayer: Dear Lord Jesus, give us generous hearts that can find as much happiness in the joys of others as in our own joys. Amen.

Grace for the Week:

We thank You, dear Lord Jesus,
For special Christmas fare,
But help us to remember
All those whose board is bare.
                    Amen.

Monday:

Reading: Luke 2: 1–3.

Thought: Christians should set an example in keeping the laws of the land.

Prayer: Dear God, help us to be honest in keeping the laws of our land because to break them is dishonouring to You. Amen.

Tuesday:

Reading: Luke 2: 4–7.

Thought: Is there room for Jesus inside our hearts?

Prayer: Come into our hearts, Lord Jesus, there is room in our hearts for Thee. Amen.

Wednesday:

Reading: Luke 2: 8–12.

Thought: Have we heard the glorious news?

Prayer: Dear Lord Jesus, give us ready ears to hear the Christmas message of Your love to men. Amen.

Thursday (Christmas Eve):

Reading: Luke 2: 13–14.

Thought: Only God sends real peace.

Prayer: Dear God, Who alone can send true peace into the hearts of men, teach us to live at peace with each other, and with those we meet each day. Amen.

Friday (Christmas Day):

Reading: Luke 2: 15–17.

Thought: Do we tell everyone the Christmas message?

Prayer: Dear Lord Jesus, today is Your birthday. Thank You for coming to the earth to save us from our sins. Help us to spread the Christmas message in some way today. Amen.

Saturday:

Reading: Luke 2: 18–20.

Thought: Will we go back to work "praising"?

Prayer: Lord Jesus Christ, when we return to work and school, fill our hearts with praise for the wonder of the Christmas story. Amen.

Sunday:

Reading: Matthew 2: 1–2 and 11.

Thought: What gifts can we bring to Jesus?

Prayer: Dear Lord Jesus, we offer to You today the gifts of ourselves. Use us and all that we have for Your Glory. Amen.